Facing Civil or Military Criminal Charges?

What to Expect and How to Deal with It

Patrick J. McLain

Speakeasy Publishing

73-03 Bell Blvd, #10

Oakland Gardens, NY 11364

www.speakeasypublishinginc.com

Ordering Information:

Quantity sales. Special discounts are available on quantity purchases by corporations, associations, and others. For details, contact the publisher at the address above.

Orders by U.S. trade bookstores and wholesalers. Please contact Speakeasy Publishing: Tel: (888) 991-2766 or visit www.speakeasypublishinginc.com.

Printed in the United States of America

Published in 2019

ISBN: 978-1-951149-10-9

FOREWORD

Who should use this Guidebook?

Any American who is being accused of a crime.

Anyone who is family or good friend to someone accused of committing a crime.

Anyone serving in the U.S. military who is facing accusations of misconduct or adverse legal action.

Anyone who is family or friend to someone serving in the U.S. military and that person is facing accusations of misconduct or adverse legal action.

How should this Guidebook be used?

Read it from cover to cover. This Guidebook is meant to be a practical help to those needing legal guidance, concise and with great clarity, and brief, to respect your time. Then give us a call. Our phone number is given three pages from this page. You can also go to our website and fill out a contact form if you want us to make the call to you.

DEDICATION

This Guidebook is dedicated to the children whom my wife Yunyong and I have raised in our forty years of marriage:

Sean and his wife Surya and son Amartya

Gabriel and his wife Lauren and daughter Kethry

Michael

Brigitte

Natalie

Catie

Sophie

Fiona and her wife Aisha

Patrick James

Isabelle

Their good lives and characters are testament to having a wonderful mother and a father who must have done something right. They have made life worth living.

Know thy self, know thy enemy. A thousand battles, a thousand victories. Victorious warriors win first and then go to war, while defeated warriors go to war first and then seek to win.

—Sun Tzu, *The Art of War*

DISCLAIMER

This publication is intended to be used for educational purposes only. No legal advice is being given, and no attorney-client relationship is intended to be created by reading this material. The author assumes no liability for any errors or omissions or for how this book or its contents are used or interpreted or for any consequences resulting directly or indirectly from the use of this book. For legal or any other advice, please consult an experienced attorney or the appropriate expert who is aware of the specific facts of your case and is knowledgeable of the law in your jurisdiction.

Law Office of Patrick J. McLain, PLLC
900 Jackson Street
Suite 640
Dallas, TX 75202
(214) 416-9100
www.patrickjmclain.com

Testimonials

"I would highly recommend Patrick McLain, to anyone needing professional representation. He's a no-nonsense attorney, that didn't sugar coat anything for me, I felt that he was truthful and honest as the day was long. His staff was very courteous and responsive, to all my calls and e-mails. The verdict is still out on my case, but I will say that if the judge listened to his closing augment, that he knocked it outta the park."

— ***Eddy S.***

****

"Patrick McLain stuck by my side for 8 long months during my case in which I was accused of violation of Article 112a. I was ultimately given a trial by Special Court Martial and thanks to his superb defense I received a Not Guilty verdict. Throughout the entire process, he never tired and always kept me focused on the task at hand."

— ***Austin W.***

****

"I hired Patrick to help out with an issue that involved my husband who is in Navy and stationed in Japan. I was worried, scared and confused, but Patrick and his staff were honest, helpful, patient and kind during this ordeal I was unexpectedly dealing with regarding my husband. Patrick got me information about my husband, his location and what he was being charged with very quickly and guided us toward the best action possible. His office is upfront with the fees you will be responsible for and they make the payment process very easy for you. They will also answer your questions (even if there are a lot of them). My husband received a very good outcome in his case and is still in the Navy. I know without a doubt it is because we had Patrick as our lawyer. While I wish that this all had never happened, hiring Patrick as our lawyer was the smartest thing I did."

— S.S.

****

"As a TCU professor, I was facing trumped-up charges in a hostile media frenzy. Patrick was part of my defense team. He was compassionate and effective. All of the charges went away. Patrick is a skilled criminal defense advocate and a good human being."

— Anonymous

****

"I have spent months trying to write this. How do you write a review for Patrick J. McLain? This man saved my life and the words on this paper just don't seem enough. I hired Patrick on November 2010 when I was charged with a capital crime in Texas. He presented himself as a professional, confident, understanding man. He discussed the law, the charges and what the next months and years would hold before trial. With no guarantee he said WE WILL WIN THIS CASE, he maintained this for 2 ½ years. In March 2013, after a 4 ½ day trial, the jury returned a verdict of NOT GUILTY. Patrick J McLain has the undying support of his office staff and most of all his family. They stand with him in all he does in life and for all he does for his clients. Patrick has truly become a good friend and if anyone needs an attorney that will stand with you during your time of trouble, look no further. Patrick J. McLain is this man."

— Child Abuse Client

****

"From day one Patrick will be on your side and make sure you are informed every step of the way. He will fight for you and present all the options good and bad so that you are fully aware of the circumstances surrounding your case. He will listen and do what you tell him to do and his staff will work their hardest for you."

— Sean O.

****

"I was a client of Patrick, and he went above and beyond for meeting my needs, as well as my family's needs. He would adjust his schedule to communicate within Japan or my wife in the States. He analyzed my case and because of his experience and expertise, he was able to help achieve the most beneficial outcome for my family and I. He is an excellent lawyer who gives his all for you and gets things done. He has a no-nonsense approach that gets you results."

— Scott S.

****

"Patrick was a wonderful lawyer his team was so kind and courtesy. Whenever I had a question and needed to talk to someone about my case I could pick up the phone and call Patrick or the office and get the help I needed. I called other offices before deciding on Patrick and all they cared about was the money. Patrick works with on a payment plan. The few time I was late on a payment Patrick work with and totally understood. You will not go wrong with Patrick and his team on your side."

— Anonymous

****

TABLE OF CONTENTS

About The Author

I started my legal career in the Marines. My first trial was in a tent in the desert in Saudi Arabia and 15 of my 20 years in the United States Marine Corps were spent in a courtroom, either as a prosecutor, a defense attorney, or a military judge. I have since retired from the Marine Corps and gone to work as a federal prosecutor. I left that practice to follow something closer to my heart, which is defending people in court and helping them restore their lives and reputations.

I am an attorney, who fights for people when the government is coming after them. I represent those charged with crimes, particularly in Texas, though some of my federal criminal work has gone beyond Texas. I also fight for military personnel, both in courts-martial as well as administrative proceedings, which can mean anything from administrative separation boards to security clearance issues. Now, my practice has started to take on civil rights cases, particularly those related to my criminal law practice, where people are harmed or treated unjustly by law enforcement personnel.

Who Is This Book For?

Over 30 years of practicing law, the same questions always pop up from my clients. This book will answer many of those questions. I know I could be helpful to anyone who is facing possible charges or if someone they care about is facing possible charges. They want to understand how the process works and what they can do to best help themselves or help loved ones. I aim to educate people, as someone who has been inside the process and tried hundreds of cases.

CHAPTER 1

WILL YOU TAKE MY CASE?

We don't ever exclude anyone. If you call with a matter of law that falls under something we can handle, whether it's criminal or military law, we're going to try to help you. Our typical clients are those who work very hard throughout their lives and want to prevent an allegation of misconduct from ruining all they've worked to achieve. Our cases tend to be federal cases or felony cases in state court, but we will listen to you, even if your charge is not of that magnitude. If we can help you, we will. If not, we'll direct you to an attorney we trust.

I Was Arrested And Charged With A Crime. What Are My Rights While I'm Under Arrest?

You always have the right to remain silent and you should always use that right.

Your only obligation, when confronted by law enforcement, is to give your identity.

You never have to agree to a search and you should never do so. If you are presented with what appears to be a search warrant, you should not get in the way of law enforcement officers who are conducting the search. You do have the right to request that law enforcement officers show proof of their identity as law enforcement officers, if they're not in uniform, and you have the right to examine any search warrant they claim they are executing. You also always have the right to film or record officers, as they do their jobs, for possible use later.

Can I Meet Or Speak To My Attorney Before I'm Questioned By Police?

Other than giving your identity, you're not obligated to give any information to law enforcement.

If you are in custody, as a civilian, they must inform you of that right and must inform you of your right to consult with an attorney. Typically, if you invoke your right to an attorney, they will cease questioning and go about finishing the rest of their business at the alleged crime scene.

It does not do you any good to talk to the police or investigators. You will not explain an accusation away, ever. You will not talk your way out of trouble. If you are being questioned, you are already a suspect, and that fact colors everything that the interrogator hears. You must always assume that the person who's interrogating you believes you to be guilty of something and therefore, they're not there to gather information to help you.

Human communication has three barriers to accurate information gathering: defects in listening, defects in memory, and defects in repeating back what was purportedly heard and remembered. If two people witness an event, you are likely to get at least three versions of that event in the retelling. It's not that you're going to give information that admits to wrongdoing; it's that what you say will never come back to you accurately. The person doing the questioning never thinks of you as possibly innocent of the accusation, so you are not speaking to an open-minded, fair audience.

"Patrick McLain is a powerful advocate for his clients. He works hard to be the very best he can be to fight for his clients. I would take any advice he has on facing allegations of misconduct."

— Betsy K. Greene

Attorney At Law, Greene & Schultz Trial Lawyers

Governor, American Association for Justice

Director, Indiana Trial Lawyers Association

Chapter 2

Should I Hire An Attorney Early On, If I'm A Suspect?

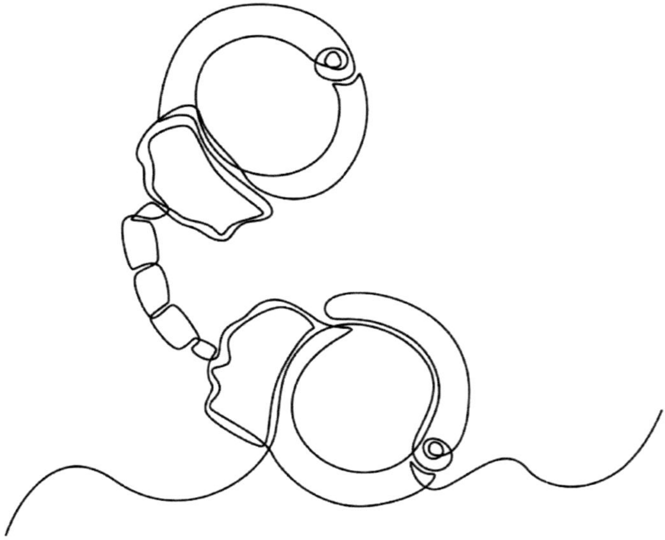

You should always consult an attorney when you are a suspect or when you suspect you are a suspect. You are definitely a suspect, if you're arrested.

An attorney will explain the system, your options, and the best course of action. This will give you the control that comes from knowledge and the comfort that comes from having a plan. It is always a wise idea to get advice from a professional and the only professional in this situation is an attorney who practices criminal law.

Will Hiring An Attorney Before I'm Arrested Make Me Look Guilty?

To quote a current TV show, Better Call Saul, "Hiring an attorney doesn't make you look guilty. Wearing handcuffs makes you look guilty."

Hiring an attorney means only one thing: you are smart enough to know that you cannot handle this on your own. Getting an attorney does not make you look guilty any more than hiring a plumber makes you look like you broke the sink.

Of course, you may be the cause of a problem, whether it's the broken sink or your legal situation, but many times, bad things happen to good people.

This is not the time to worry about your image. This is the time to start fixing a problem that you have.

What Should I Look For When Hiring A Criminal Defense Attorney?

You must have a clearly defined goal in your legal situation to give to the attorney. An attorney cannot promise results; that is neither ethical nor legal. The attorney needs to know how this legal situation is affecting your life.

The Law Office of Patrick J McLain takes a personal approach to legal problem solving and you will be expected to be open, honest, and accurate with our attorneys and staff. They will always be so with you.

It is important, when you're hiring a criminal attorney, that you find one who listens. If all you hear from the attorney is about the attorney and what he has done, you can be assured that what a man talks about most, he does not have. The attorney should be doing most of the listening because only by listening to you and getting information can the attorney give you sound advice.

It's important that you allow the attorney to move the discussion in the direction in which he can be helpful. The things you think are important may not be immediately important to the attorney who is helping you. Be patient and allow the attorney to guide the discussion, even if it is primarily a listening exercise on the part of the attorney.

How Often Should I Expect To Meet With My Attorney And Will I Receive Regular Updates On My Criminal Case?

Work that your attorney does on your case in front of you is like the tip of an iceberg. There is a whole team working in the background as well Most of the work does not involve seeing the client. You should expect to be regularly updated but you should never feel that you have to wait for that call.

At the Law Office of Patrick J McLain, we have an around-the-clock answering service and we will contact you the next business day, if the answering service advises us that you have an emergency. The degree of contact you can expect will vary depending on the nature of the case.

Once I Have An Attorney, What Can I Do To Help My Attorney Defend My Criminal Case?

You are a vital part of the process.

You are the master of the facts, just as your attorney is the master of the law.

You're going to work with the attorney who is on your contract, whether it is Patrick J McLain or another attorney in our law office. You will be expected to give narratives, work up reenactments of the facts, and help build the witness list for your legal proceeding. If your case is a criminal matter, you make the big decisions, with our advice, on issues like pleas, whether a judge or a jury will be the decider of your case, and whether or not you will testify.

You will also be asked to work with any other attorneys or staff who are assigned to your case. At Patrick J McLain's law firm, they are all well-trained and as devoted to your case and its success as your lead attorney is. It will be made clear to you, before you sign up and pay your legal fee, who is the lead attorney on your case and how the process works.

"Patrick McLain relentlessly bridges the gap-of-despair for those in need! He is more than an advocate---He is a Warrior for Justice! Patrick McLain is a compassionate advocate who cares for others----He is a resounding voice for the voiceless, a ray of hope for the downtrodden, and a healer for the hurting! Patrick McLain- In a world full of division—He is TRUST when you need it most. Patrick McLain is an authentic champion for those finding themselves in troubled waters. His courtroom expertise, skill, and passion CHANGE lives for the BETTER! Patrick McLain- When push comes to shove and the stakes are high, you need an advocate with the HEART OF A LION. You need Patrick McLain!

— Bill Pickett

Trial Lawyer

Past President, State Bar of Washington

CHAPTER 3

WHAT SHOULD YOU EXPECT AFTER YOUR ARREST?

If you hire an attorney before there's an arrest warrant, such as the attorneys from the Law Office of Patrick J McLain, they can do everything in our power to avoid law enforcement coming to your home or your workplace to arrest you. Patrick J McLain will endeavor to work out a voluntary turn-in. You can appear at the courthouse, have a bond set, if necessary, and we can return you to your life while your legal case is pending.

If you have already been arrested, there will be a series of hearings, leading up to trial or the resolution of your case.

In state court, the schedule can be long and drawn out.

In federal court, a trial is quickly set for 70 days after the arrest.

Usually, there are one or two continuances, or delays, before the case is resolved by trial or other means.

Military courts tend to move the fastest with set schedules, which only change due to unforeseen events.

Should I Get Counseling Or Treatment Relating To My Charges While My Case Is Ongoing?

Your mental and physical health is important at all times, especially when you're facing so stressful a situation as serious criminal charges. You should always consult your attorney for the best way to get counseling or treatment and still protect your legal rights.

At the Law Office of Patrick J McLain, we always want you to be in the best health, physically and mentally, because that helps us better serve you.

After My Arrest, How Soon Am I Going To Have A First Court Date?

Your court dates can be as often as once a month or several months apart.

This varies widely between jurisdictions. Every state, federal, and military court does things the way that particular judge chooses to have them done. Often, judges or prosecutors have served a long time in a certain court and have a hard time understanding that things are done differently in other courts.

The job of your attorney is to learn and adjust for those local differences, so that you are always protected.

Do I Need To Attend All My Court Appearances Or Could My Attorney Do So On My Behalf?

In federal and military courts, you will have to be present at all your hearings.

In state courts, depending on the local judge's rules, you may not have to show up for status hearings or similar events. State court criminal proceedings tend to have a lot more hearings in court before resolution.

If I Am Overseas Or Out Of State At The Time Of My Criminal Or Military Court Dates, Is That An Excusable Absence?

Military personnel facing charges in a state or federal court must be requested by the court through the military person's chain of command. Ordinarily, the military commander will cooperate by assuring the attendance of military persons to their court hearings.

The only common exception to this rule is the case of military personnel assigned to a combat post. Then, the military commander will normally ask the court to delay the proceeding until the military person has returned from combat and that person will be made available for the legal proceeding in civilian court.

"Patrick McLain is a true warrior in and out of the courtroom. As a Major in the Marine Corp, he did his level best to help his Marines. He has done the same for service men and women across the globe, relentlessly defending their liberty in military and civilian courts. He's guided by his faith and his humanity. When everything is on the line, he's the one you want with you in court. There is simply no better criminal defense attorney anywhere."

— Robert Persante, Esq.
Persante Zuroweste, P.A.
Florida Estate, Trust & Securities

CHAPTER 4

AT WHAT POINT WILL WE SEE EVIDENCE?

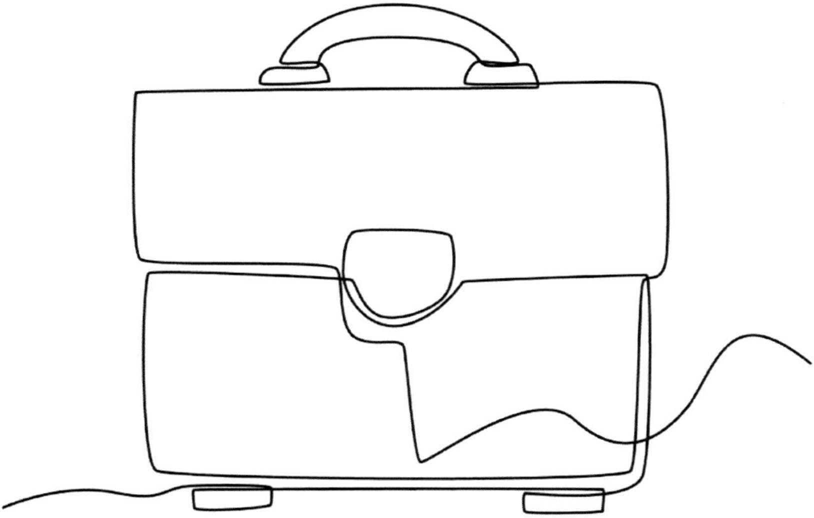

You will not see any evidence, also known as discovery, against you until you are charged.

The timeframe for the discovery process varies by jurisdiction. In Texas, thanks to a law called the Michael Morton Act, prosecutors in state courts are required to give discovery early and completely.

There is no such guarantee in federal court. Usually, the federal prosecutor will initially give your defense attorney only so much evidence, in the hopes of inducing an offer to plead guilty. It is only when your attorney makes it clear to the federal prosecutor that he is serious about seeking a trial that the federal prosecutor will give more complete discovery. Even then, it has been my experience that federal prosecutors hold onto discovery for as long as they can before they turn it over to the defense.

The military has a much more open discovery practice.

At What Point In The Case Will My Lawyer Enter My Plea Of Guilty Or Not Guilty? Will We Have All Of The Evidence Before I Have To Make A Plea?

The attorney only enters a plea on your behalf. You are the sole decider of how you're going to plead.

Your attorney should always enter a plea of not guilty, on your behalf, at your arraignment. The arraignment is an early hearing in which the court makes sure you know the charges, have an attorney, and that a schedule is set. You should never plead guilty until you have looked at the government's evidence and studied what evidence your attorney has found.

You always have the legal right to plead not guilty and require the government to prove its case against you, if it can, through legal and competent evidence, beyond a reasonable doubt.

If you did not commit the crime you're accused of, you should always plead not guilty and never change to guilty.

Even if you are guilty, if you think that the evidence will not prevail or you simply wish to plead not guilty, you have every legal right to do so.

"Even the accusation of having done wrong can be devastating and disruptive to the accused. These allegations invade nearly every thought and deprive the accused person of sleep, peace, and sometimes hope. When a champion steps up to defend against that accusation, a ray of that lost hope returns. When Patrick McLain is that ray, it can often open a wide beam of justice. He has brought the light and hope back to so many that he must have lost count. "

— L. Todd Kelly

Senior Partner, The Kelly Law Firm, P.C.

Author "Worth Dying For" and "The Power Within"

CHAPTER 5

EXPERTS THAT CAN BE USED TO BUILD A DEFENSE

Your attorney should have a good mastery of the law and should also know his or her limitations. If understanding the facts in your case requires the assistance of an expert in medicine, mental health, forensics, or any other specialized field, your attorney should be wise and humble enough to seek that assistance.

Unless you are in the military or your attorney is court-appointed, you will have to pay for the expert help. You will be involved in the decision-making for hiring any experts, and will have to approve the expense.

There is hardly a field of expertise that has not come into play in a criminal case, at some point.

We have used experts in accident reconstruction, analysis of fiber and DNA, mental health, and even religion. There is no limitation to the type of experts who may be necessary for the defense.

When Might Prosecutors Offer A Plea Deal And What To Expect As A First-Time Offender?

The timing of a plea deal varies widely between courts.

Prosecutors do not have to make plea offers at all. In most state and federal jurisdictions, the prosecutor will give an initial offer for a plea deal. This offer will usually be subject to change, as the legal process moves forward. There also comes a time when a prosecutor will lose interest in making a plea deal, especially if the prosecutor has already put in a lot of work and preparation for trial.

It is up to your attorney to know the best timing for a plea deal, if you wish to seek such a resolution.

"Patrick's tireless commitment to his clients, unsurpassed advocacy skills and passion for justice sets Patrick aside from other lawyers. He has a unique ability to look through and beyond raw facts and get to the substance of the client's story. He then presents that story in ways that it is ultimately received by open minds, yielding amazing and just results."

— Kenny Adair

Former US Navy Petty Officer

Trial Lawyer

Retired Oklahoma District Judge

CHAPTER 6

WHAT TO EXPECT IF YOU DECIDE TO FIGHT THE CHARGES

If you take your case to trial, you can expect that there will be a trial schedule set, which will give you an idea of how long it will take to get to court.

State cases usually have multiple settings and federal courts usually have one or two delays in the originally published schedule.

Be prepared for a long fight. Time is often your ally as a defendant in a criminal case.

You have to leave it to the experience and expertise of your criminal defense attorney to know when to strike and when to delay.

Factors To Consider Before You Decide To Take A Plea Offer Or Fight Charges

You should never plead guilty, if you did not commit the crime.

You must tell your attorney the truth, including whether or not you committed the act. An attorney cannot, ethically, bring you to court to plead guilty to something that you're telling him you did not do. Your attorney is not there to judge you. He or she is working for you to keep you from being judged too severely. The only way your attorney can help you is if you give them complete and accurate information.

If you have held back from your attorney the whole truth, you should never be so embarrassed about that as to give up a good and fair plea deal.

Even if you committed the act alleged, if it appears that the government cannot prove its case against you, you may wish to plead not guilty, and that is likely the best course of action.

A defense attorney cannot and should not be trying to dissuade you from a not guilty plea, but it is also his duty to advise you of the consequences of any choice you make.

If I Am Convicted, Will My Sentence Be More Severe Than The Original Plea Offer?

Sometimes, a guilty plea may get you lenience. The criminal justice system eschews any punishment for exercising a right to a trial. While you have a right to a trial, that doesn't mean that you won't get some extra lenience if you plead guilty.

Your punishment, however, should never be based on your exercising a legal right, including a right to a trial on the facts.

MARINE CO

"Patrick McLain is one of the hardest-working lawyers I know — and I know a lot of lawyers. His approach to the practice of law is not only thorough and technically adept, but emotionally intelligent and wise. He tries cases all over the world and he tries more cases in a year than most lawyers do in an entire career. The advice he offers in this book will help anyone facing accusations to find the best approach to deal with them."

— Andrew B. Delaney

Past President, Vermont Association for Justice

President Elect, F Warriors (alumni association of the Trial Lawyers College)

CHAPTER 7

WHEN DOES SENTENCING OCCUR IN A CRIMINAL OR MILITARY CASE?

If there is going to be sentencing, when that sentence is decided varies widely from criminal court to criminal court.

In military courts, if you're convicted, the case goes to sentencing right away. In federal court, sentencing happens about four months after conviction, after the federal judge receives their pre-sentence report from the court's probation officers. In state courts, if it's trial by jury, the jury will decide a sentence soon after the guilty finding, usually the same day or the following day.

The government and defense will both present evidence supporting their sentencing recommendations. If your sentence in state court is going to be decided by a judge, there may be a time when they want their probation officer to do research and give recommendations.

Sentencing Guidelines For Misdemeanor And Felony Convictions

General sentencing guidelines can provide required minimum and mandatory maximum sentences, which the sentencing authority cannot go beyond. Whether or not an offense has a set minimum or maximum sentence, there's always a wide range of possible punishments that can be given.

In many jurisdictions, having multiple convictions can increase your sentence.

It is important that your attorney prepares well for sentencing. If your case looks simple and straightforward, you should support your attorney in putting together the best sentencing case possible, which is based upon the evidence presented to the court. This is evidence in addition to what has already been presented in the case in which your guilt was decided.

ARMY
ARMY
IRON

"Patrick is a tireless advocate whose passion, compassion, dedication, perseverance, and creativity in the defense of his clients produces outstanding and impressive results."

— Kristin A. Ross, Esq.

Rousseau & Ross, PLLC

President of the Vermont Association for Justice

Past President, New Hampshire Association for Justice

Chapter 8

Factors You Should Consider When Hiring An Attorney

You should hire an attorney who listens and hears what you have to say. An attorney who tells you all about himself and his accomplishments is selling you, rather than helping you. Your attorney should be brutally honest with you and tell you what you need to know, not what you want to hear. He or she should give you hope by discussing possibilities with you and talking about options that may give you the best possible chance to get your life back.

Any attorney who can talk all day with you, without being paid, is likely either lacking clients or does not give his paying clients the time they need on their cases. Put yourself in the shoes of someone who has hired this attorney and know that it would be a concern to you if this attorney spent long hours talking with people who have not hired him, when you have paid him to work long and hard on your case. For most attorneys, the initial consultation is going to be focused and time-limited.

Hire Someone Who Has Specific Experience As a Prosecutor Or As A Judge

You do not have to have served as a prosecutor or a judge to be a good criminal defense attorney, but it helps if you use that experience to understand your opponent in the courtroom. In order to get helpful information from a witness, another attorney, or a judge, an attorney must first be a good listener and be able to understand the role of that person and where they're coming from. The loud and bragging attorney does not win cases. It is the quiet, compassionate, dedicated attorney, who listens to others and understands them, who prevails in the fight.

What Does A Full-Service Defense Attorney In Practice Mean?

When working with a full-service defense firm, you will be expected to be fully engaged in your defense. You and your future are what this whole legal process is about. You should always be treated with respect. The attorneys and staff should always look for ways to be engaged with you, so that they have the best chance of getting a good result.

"When I think of Patrick's advocacy I feel compassion and determination to be there for his client. Patrick treats everyone he encounters with compassion and love. Patrick is a gentle yet fearless giant in the Courtroom."

— Harry L. Daniels, III

Partner, Daniels & Washington Law Firm, L.L.C.

Trial Lawyer, Baton Rouge, Louisiana

CHAPTER 9

WHAT IF I'M A MILITARY PERSON AND CHARGED WITH A CRIME?

Theoretically, any service member could face additional military prosecution for alleged misconduct when facing state criminal charges for the same alleged act. Federal cases, however, are limited by a concept called dual sovereignty. Almost always, you will be facing only one criminal judicial proceeding.

If you are pending criminal charges in a civilian court, as a military person, you will likely face administrative separation or show cause and you will need an expert in military law.

Consequences Of A Conviction For Your Military Career

A conviction in civilian court will almost certainly be addressed by an administrative separation proceeding, if you're enlisted, or a show-cause proceeding, if you're an officer. You can and should have an attorney representing you during these hearings, just like any judicial proceeding.

Your participation in gathering evidence to present in your case is vital. These are proceedings in which good preparation and experience are essential to a good result because if they don't go your way, they could result in the loss of your career or retirement.

Do You Represent And Defend Military Members In All Service Branches?

The Law Office of Patrick J McLain represents military persons in all branches, all over the world. We have represented the Guardians (Space Force) along with Soldiers, Sailors, Airmen, Marines, and Coast Guard personnel throughout Europe, Asia, the Middle East, and all parts of the United States and its territories. We go to our clients wherever they live and work. There is not a military base in the world that we cannot go to fight for their rights.

As A Member Of The Military, I Was Offered A Defense Attorney. Should I Decline The Military Attorney And Work With A Civilian Attorney?

You should always keep your military counsel, even when you hire a civilian counsel. It is your right and you should always fully exercise your rights.

You should hire a civilian counsel because that attorney provides a better chance for you to get a good result because of their experience and proven track record. The local military attorney is an invaluable resource for your case preparation, presentation, and for working as a team player with the civilian counsel. Sometimes, you are assigned a military attorney with whom you cannot work well. You have the right to request a military attorney of your own selection, provided that military attorney is reasonably available.

Can I Meet With Or Speak To My Attorney Before I'm Questioned By Military Investigators?

In the military, you have the same right to silence that civilians have. Persons subject to the Uniform Code of Military Justice, in which all military personnel and all persons investigated from the military, must be read their rights to be silent and to consult an attorney.

Law enforcement only has to do this with civilians, if the civilian is in custody, but all persons who are subject to the criminal code in the military must be read those rights, advising them that they can be silent and may consult an attorney before making that decision, even if they have not been arrested.

What to Expect When You Are Charged With A Crime And Released in the Military Justice System?

If you have been arrested and released, immediately seek legal advice from an attorney at the local military defense counsel office. Get the advice of that military counsel and consulting civilian counsel. Gather all the advice you can get.

Getting advice from more than one attorney is always a wise decision.

Should I Really Hire a Civilian Attorney To Assist With A Military Case?

I practiced military law as an officer in the Marine Corps for 15 years and I've been in the practice of military law, as a civilian attorney, for over 15 years. I have many assets available to allow me to build a good case for my military clients, including working with the military defense counsel.

When Will My Lawyer Enter My Plea Of Guilty Or Not Guilty In My Military Case? Will We Have All The Evidence Before I Make That Plea?

"You must never enter a plea of guilty or not guilty in a military case until you have gone over all the evidence with your attorney." In the military, the discovery of evidence is very open and the government lawyers are required to give all their evidence to the defense early and often. The military justice system contains protections for the rights of the accused that are higher than in the civilian system.

"Patrick McLain is a Warrior for Justice! Regardless of your circumstances, he will fight for you and your cause like a true Marine fighting with his last breath to save his fellow troops and Country. He has achieved his remarkable success with passion and grace. It is my privilege to teach fellow trial lawyers with him and to call him a friend."

— Mark Wagner
Trial Lawyer
Tacoma, Washington

CHAPTER 10

WHAT IS THE COURT-MARTIAL PROCEDURE?

Only certain commanders can convene courts-martial. When a commander sees a report of alleged misconduct and they decide a judicial proceeding is most appropriate, the commander refers the matter to a court-martial. The proceeding is then assigned to a military judge, who takes charge of the scheduling and administration of the case.

Military judges work independently of commanders and cannot terminate a court-martial. However, military judges can indefinitely suspend or abate court-martial proceedings to make sure that the government acts in a fair manner.

I know this well, as a former military judge, since I required trial counsel and commanders provide the accused military person had a fair and just trial.

What Is The Article 32 Hearing And What Do I Hope To Accomplish At Article 32?

Under Article 32 of the Uniform Code of Military Justice, this hearing is a pre-trial investigation that must consider whether there is probable cause to support a charge before it can be sent to the highest level of a judicial proceeding, known as a general court-martial.

Though it is not the purpose of the Article 32 hearing to provide discovery to the defense, this is often the natural result. The defense gets valuable information about the case from this pre-trial investigation hearing.

Is it the rough equivalent of a grand jury hearing, in the civilian world? It is a screening process to make sure that when you have serious charges, the process has a second look before proceeding.

Why Patrick J McLain Is The Natural Fit For A Military Member Who Is Facing Criminal Charges?

I went to a great law school and I fought in one of the purest and best-staffed justice systems in the country, the military justice system.

I have tried hundreds of cases as a defense attorney, hundreds as a prosecutor, and hundreds as a judge.

People come to me because they have worked hard in life to get where they are and they see it all threatened by this criminal charge. They're looking to us to fight to help restore their life to the way it was before the criminal charge.

I think what they see in me is hard work, dedication, and loyalty, which is what Semper Fidelis, the motto of the Marine Corps, means. We will always stand by them in the fight.

Can Or Should Any Criminal Defense Attorney Handle Military Cases?

I would not advise anyone who has not been in military court to try to defend a military case. The proceedings and the language are different. The community values and ethos are different. You have to understand the military person.

Having served 20 years in the Marines, it's immediately apparent to my clients, to my opponents, and to the judges that I understand the culture well.

Is There Anything Else That Sets Patrick J McLain Apart?

You could be a great criminal defense attorney without having been a prosecutor or a judge. However, being a former prosecutor or judge makes you more effective in the fight, because you have been in their job.

More than experience, clients should want to know whether you care about them. They want to get the feeling that you care enough about their case.

A person who has to brag about all that he's accomplished is usually insecure, and probably for good reason.

I care for my clients, and it shows at trial. I recall being in federal court where the judge hated me and my techniques. I still got a not guilty verdict because the jury loved me.

They could see that I was telling them the truth; that I cared about my client, and that I was real.

That's what a client should want, in the end. They want to know that you've listened to them, you know their story, and you're going to tell it with conviction, so that the jury will see the truth.

Degrees and plaques on the wall don't get you sincerity. I've got tons of experience, but a client is well-served to look deeper than that.

"Never Meet Your Heroes" hits harder every birthday, especially after 20 years watching the betrayals of our criminal justice system as a practitioner. Patrick McLain remains the exception and proves to this limited believer that higher powers are at work. Without qualification, no other single advocate has done more for the warriors fighting for justice (lawyers and clients) than Patrick McLain. Teaching, practicing, leading and doing the WORK, Patrick is a model of aspiration for all Justice Seekers."

— Joshua Schiffer, Esq.

Attorney-at-Law and legal analyst on Court TV

ChancoSchiffer – Georgia – US Virgin Islands

What Is The Next Step?

The Law Office of Patrick J. McLain, PLLC represents clients who have been accused of or charged with serious state and federal crimes throughout the Dallas area.

Whether you are facing felony drug charges, have been arrested for DWI, or believe you are under investigation for fraud, embezzlement, or any other white-collar crime, you have the constitutional right to be presumed innocent unless proven guilty beyond a reasonable doubt. Our Dallas criminal defense lawyers are prepared to fight tirelessly to ensure that your rights are protected.

Call (214) 416-9100 or visit www.patrickjmclain.com to discuss your charges, as well as the best course of action with our criminal defense attorneys in Dallas.

ACKNOWLEDGEMENTS

This book, like much in my life, was a family effort. Brigitte lead the effort to write, edit, and produce this guidebook. Michael worked for me for about a decade, and his patient efforts to improve our work to support, and fight for, our clients has resulted in a much better law office. Natalie has brought a great deal of practical wisdom and common sense to the way we maintain records and achieve the best results for our clients.

Sean helped me get my law practice launched in 2004. Fiona has been there at critical times to help her siblings and me handle the necessary, and occasionally burdensome, tasks that must be done to help our clients. Gabriel, Catie, Sophie, Patrick James, and Isabelle provided their lawyer father help with tasks as needed or even a base of operations, be it in Tucson or in Tokyo, as I have taken my law practice all over the world, quite literally.

Finally, my wife Yunyong has surely earned a plenary indulgence in her four decades of marriage to man who is an unrepentant work addict in his fight for justice.

NOTES

Made in United States
Orlando, FL
04 November 2026

90208510R00048